C000082723

# Super Simple Spanish

### Basic & Essential Spanish Words

Des Meagher

Beverley Roberts

Super Simple Spanish ™

This edition first published in 2008.

ISBN 13  978-0-9552198-3-2

Printed and bound in Spain
by Gráficas San Pancracio, S.L.
www.gspimpresores.com

For more information about the
Super Simple Spanish series
please see our website:

www.supersimplespanish.com

# Contents

# The Authors

We've been visiting Spain together
for more than twenty years.
In 1997 we spent a year in Spain
travelling around the country,
enjoying the Spanish way of life
and trying to learn Spanish.

We moved to Spain in 1998 and
spent several years teaching
English in Madrid and Seville.
Our teaching experience plus our
own attempts to learn Spanish
convinced us that most of the books
on the market are far too complicated.

We decided to write a series of books
that would make learning Spanish as
simple as possible.

# Introduction

Super Simple Spanish books are designed to make Spanish as simple as possible.

Basic and Essential Words gives you:

## Spanish Words
Over 1400 basic and essential words grouped together under 100 simple headings.

## Spanish Sounds
The most important sounds in Spanish pronunciation and how word stress is used in Spanish.

## Spain
The highlights of Spain with maps of mainland Spain and the Spanish islands.

# Super Simple Spanish

Super Simple Spanish is a series of books designed to make Spanish as simple as possible.

Each book in the series gives you important Spanish words, simple Spanish pronunciation and our guide to the highlights of Spain.

The first 2 books in this series are:

## Identical and Similar Words
Over 1200 Spanish words.
Every word is identical or very similar in English.

## Basic and Essential Words
Over 1400 basic and essential Spanish words grouped together under 100 simple headings.

# SPANISH WORDS

## Basic Spanish Words

## Essential Spanish Words A-Z

# PLEASE NOTE

The Spanish Words section has many Spanish words that end in **o**. Words ending in **o** are usually masculine in Spanish.

There are also many words that end in **a** in Spanish and these words are usually feminine.

Some Spanish words can end in **o** or **a** if they are used in the masculine and the feminine. For example,

amig**o**  = male friend
amig**a**  = female friend

camarer**o** = waiter
camarer**a** = waitress

To keep the Spanish Words section as simple as possible we have used the masculine ending **o** for words that can be used in the masculine and the feminine.

# THE BASICS

| | |
|---|---|
| yes | sí |
| no | no |
| please | por favor |
| thank you | gracias |
| okay | vale |
| excuse me | perdón |
| sorry | lo siento |
| you're welcome | de nada |

# THE BASICS

| | |
|---|---|
| hello | hola |
| good morning | buenos días |
| good afternoon | buenas tardes |
| good evening | buenas tardes |
| goodnight | buenas noches |
| goodbye | adiós |
| see you later | hasta luego |
| see you tomorrow | hasta mañana |

# THE BASICS

| | |
|---|---|
| Mr | Señor |
| Mrs | Señora |
| Miss | Señorita |
| husband | marido |
| wife | esposa |
| father | padre |
| mother | madre |
| son | hijo |
| daughter | hija |
| friend | amigo |

# THE BASICS

| | |
|---|---|
| airport | aeropuerto |
| taxi | taxi |
| bus | autobús |
| train | tren |
| underground | metro |
| ticket | billete |
| bus station | estación de autobuses |
| train station | estación de tren |

# THE BASICS

| | |
|---|---|
| bank | banco |
| money | dinero |
| coin | moneda |
| cash machine | cajero automático |
| debit card | tarjeta de débito |
| credit card | tarjeta de crédito |
| foreign exchange | cambio |

# THE BASICS

| | |
|---|---|
| tourist office | oficina de turismo |
| information | información |
| town map | plano |
| timetable | horario |
| hotel | hotel |
| restaurant | restaurante |
| toilets | servicios |
| Ladies | Señoras |
| Gents | Caballeros |

# THE BASICS

| | |
|---|---|
| town | ciudad |
| town centre | centro ciudad |
| town hall | ayuntamiento |
| main square | plaza mayor |
| street | calle |
| church | iglesia |
| park | parque |
| river | río |
| bridge | puente |
| beach | playa |

# THE BASICS

| | |
|---|---|
| shop | tienda |
| market | mercado |
| supermarket | supermercado |
| car park | parking |
| chemist's | farmacia |
| post office | Correos |
| shopping centre | centro comercial |
| department store | grandes almacenes |

# THE BASICS

| | |
|---|---|
| accident | accidente |
| police | policía |
| ambulance | ambulancia |
| fire brigade | bomberos |
| Red Cross | Cruz Roja |
| doctor | médico |
| dentist | dentista |
| hospital | hospital |
| accident & emergency | urgencias |

# THE BASICS

| | |
|---|---|
| tea | té |
| coffee | café |
| milk | leche |
| sugar | azúcar |
| drinking chocolate | chocolate en polvo |
| water | agua |
| juice | zumo |
| beer | cerveza |
| wine | vino |

# THE BASICS

| | |
|---|---|
| bread | pan |
| butter | mantequilla |
| toast | tostada |
| jam | mermelada |
| honey | miel |
| eggs | huevos |
| bacon | bacon |
| ham | jamón |
| cheese | queso |

# THE BASICS

| | |
|---|---|
| hot | caliente |
| cold | frío |
| big | grande |
| small | pequeño |
| a lot | mucho |
| a little | poco |
| more | más |
| less | menos |
| with | con |
| without | sin |

# THE BASICS

| | |
|---|---|
| one | uno |
| two | dos |
| three | tres |
| four | cuatro |
| five | cinco |
| six | seis |
| seven | siete |
| eight | ocho |
| nine | nueve |
| ten | diez |

# THE BASICS

| | |
|---|---|
| today | hoy |
| tomorrow | mañana |
| yesterday | ayer |
| now | ahora |
| soon | pronto |
| later | más tarde |
| before | antes |
| after | después |
| here | aquí |
| there | allí |

# THE BASICS

| Monday    | lunes     |
|-----------|-----------|
| Tuesday   | martes    |
| Wednesday | miércoles |
| Thursday  | jueves    |
| Friday    | viernes   |
| Saturday  | sábado    |
| Sunday    | domingo   |

# THE BASICS

| | |
|---|---|
| Where is..? | ¿Dónde está..? |
| How much..? | ¿Cuánto..? |
| What time..? | ¿A qué hora..? |
| Is there...? | ¿Hay..? |
| What's your name? | ¿Cómo se llama? |
| Where are you from? | ¿De dónde es? |
| Do you speak English? | ¿Habla inglés? |

# Essential
# Spanish
# Words
# A-Z

# AIRPORT

| | |
|---|---|
| airport | aeropuerto |
| arrivals | llegadas |
| departures | salidas |
| passport | pasaporte |
| ticket | billete |
| suitcase | maleta |
| luggage | equipaje |
| information | información |
| flight | vuelo |
| gate | puerta |
| foreign exchange | cambio |

# ANIMALS

| | |
|---|---|
| animal | animal |
| bird | ave |
| dog | perro |
| cat | gato |
| horse | caballo |
| cow | vaca |
| sheep | oveja |
| pig | cerdo |
| chicken | pollo |
| rabbit | conejo |
| bull | toro |
| goat | cabra |

# APARTMENT

| | |
|---|---|
| apartment | apartamento |
| building | edificio |
| flat | piso |
| penthouse | ático |
| floor | planta |
| lift | ascensor |
| stairs | escalera |
| balcony | balcón |
| roof terrace | azotea |
| swimming pool | piscina |
| letter-box | buzón |
| rubbish | basura |

# BABIES

| | |
|---|---|
| baby | bebé |
| milk | leche |
| bottle | biberón |
| nappy | pañal |
| wet wipes | toallitas húmedas |
| changing mat | cambiador |
| pushchair | cochecito |
| high chair | trona |
| cot | cuna |
| babysitter | canguro |
| car seat | silla de automóvil |

# BAGS

| | |
|---|---|
| bag | bolsa |
| handbag | bolso |
| purse | monedero |
| wallet | cartera |
| backpack | mochila |
| holdall | bolsa de viaje |
| beach bag | bolsa de playa |
| briefcase | maletín |
| suitcase | maleta |
| luggage | equipaje |
| hand luggage | equipaje de mano |

# THE BANK

| | |
|---|---|
| bank | banco |
| client | cliente |
| money | dinero |
| cash machine | cajero automático |
| cheque | cheque |
| transfer | transferencia |
| debit card | tarjeta de débito |
| credit card | tarjeta de crédito |
| commission | comisión |
| foreign exchange | cambio |

# THE BANK

| | |
|---|---|
| current account | cuenta corriente |
| savings account | cuenta de ahorros |
| mortgage | hipoteca |
| loan | préstamo |
| interest | interés |
| balance | saldo |
| deposit | ingreso |
| payment | pago |
| withdrawal | reintegro |
| overdraft | descubierto |

# BATHROOM

| | |
|---|---|
| bathroom | cuarto de baño |
| bath | baño |
| shower | ducha |
| toilet | aseo |
| bidet | bidé |
| sink | lavabo |
| tap | grifo |
| wall tiles | azulejos |
| mirror | espejo |
| shower curtain | cortina de ducha |
| towel | toalla |

# THE BEACH

| | |
|---|---|
| beach | playa |
| sun | sol |
| sea | mar |
| sand | arena |
| wave | ola |
| shell | concha |
| beach bar | chiringuito |
| sun lounger | hamaca |
| beach umbrella | sombrilla |
| flag | bandera |
| lifeguard | socorrista |

# BEDROOM

| | |
|---|---|
| bedroom | dormitorio |
| bed | cama |
| mattress | colchón |
| sheet | sábana |
| pillow | almohada |
| pillowcase | funda |
| duvet | edredón |
| blanket | manta |
| wardrobe | armario |
| coat hanger | percha |
| lamp | lámpara |
| alarm clock | despertador |

# BICYCLE

| | |
|---|---|
| bicycle | bicicleta |
| saddle | sillín |
| gears | marchas |
| brake | freno |
| chain | cadena |
| pedal | pedal |
| wheel | rueda |
| tyre | cubierta |
| puncture | pinchazo |
| pump | bomba |
| lock | candado |
| helmet | casco |

# THE BODY

| | |
|---|---|
| body | cuerpo |
| skin | piel |
| head | cabeza |
| neck | cuello |
| shoulder | hombro |
| back | espalda |
| chest | pecho |
| stomach | estómago |
| arm | brazo |
| leg | pierna |
| hand | mano |
| foot | pie |

# THE BODY

| | |
|---|---|
| elbow | codo |
| wrist | muñeca |
| knee | rodilla |
| ankle | tobillo |
| finger | dedo |
| toe | dedo del pie |
| face | cara |
| eye | ojo |
| ear | oreja |
| nose | nariz |
| mouth | boca |
| tooth | diente |

# CAMPING

| | |
|---|---|
| campsite | camping |
| camper | campista |
| pitch | plaza |
| tent | tienda |
| caravan | caravana |
| camper van | cámper |
| trailer | remolque |
| showers | duchas |
| electricity | electricidad |
| drinking water | agua potable |
| no vacancies | completo |

# CELEBRATIONS

| | |
|---|---|
| celebration | celebración |
| party | fiesta |
| present | regalo |
| birthday | cumpleaños |
| engagement | compromiso |
| wedding | boda |
| honeymoon | luna de miel |
| anniversary | aniversario |
| retirement | jubilación |
| congratulations | enhorabuena |
| happy birthday | feliz cumpleaños |

# CHEMIST

| | |
|---|---|
| chemist's | farmacia |
| cut | corte |
| bite | picadura |
| burn | quemadura |
| pain | dolor |
| allergy | alergia |
| nausea | náusea |
| aspirin | aspirina |
| paracetamol | paracetamol |
| antibiotic | antibiótico |
| antiseptic | antiséptico |
| plaster | tirita® |

# CLOTHES

| | |
|---|---|
| clothes | ropa |
| coat | abrigo |
| jacket | chaqueta |
| shirt | camisa |
| trousers | pantalones |
| jumper | suéter |
| blouse | blusa |
| dress | vestido |
| skirt | falda |
| shoes | zapatos |
| shorts | pantalones cortos |

# CLOTHES

| | |
|---|---|
| jeans | vaqueros |
| t-shirt | camiseta |
| belt | cinturón |
| tie | corbata |
| socks | calcetines |
| underwear | ropa interior |
| bra | sujetador |
| knickers | bragas |
| tights | medias |
| underpants | calzoncillos |
| pyjamas | pijama |
| swimwear | bañadores |

# THE COAST

| | |
|---|---|
| coast | costa |
| beach | playa |
| sea | mar |
| shore | orilla |
| dune | duna |
| rock | roca |
| cove | cala |
| bay | bahía |
| island | isla |
| cape | cabo |
| lighthouse | faro |
| cliff | acantilado |

# COLOURS

| | |
|---|---|
| colour | color |
| red | rojo |
| yellow | amarillo |
| blue | azul |
| green | verde |
| black | negro |
| white | blanco |
| grey | gris |
| pink | rosa |
| purple | morado |
| orange | naranja |
| brown | marrón |

# COMPUTERS

| | |
|---|---|
| computer | ordenador |
| keyboard | teclado |
| mouse | ratón |
| monitor | monitor |
| screen | pantalla |
| hard drive | disco duro |
| software | software |
| program | programa |
| disk | disco |
| cable | cable |
| printer | impresora |
| ink | tinta |

# COOKING

| | |
|---|---|
| cook | cocinero |
| meal | comida |
| homemade | casera |
| roast | asado |
| fried | frito |
| baked | al horno |
| grilled | a la parrilla |
| barbecued | a la brasa |
| on a hotplate | a la plancha |
| battered | a la romana |
| stuffed | relleno |
| smoked | ahumado |

# COUNTRIES

| | |
|---|---|
| country | país |
| England | Inglaterra |
| Scotland | Escocia |
| Wales | Gales |
| Northern Ireland | Irlanda del Norte |
| Ireland | Irlanda |
| Spain | España |
| Portugal | Portugal |
| France | Francia |
| Italy | Italia |
| Germany | Alemania |

# COUNTRIES

| | |
|---|---|
| United States | Estados Unidos |
| Canada | Canadá |
| Australia | Australia |
| New Zealand | Nueva Zelanda |
| Russia | Rusia |
| China | China |
| Japan | Japón |
| Holland | Holanda |
| Belgium | Bélgica |
| Norway | Noruega |
| Sweden | Suecia |
| Denmark | Dinamarca |

# COUNTRYSIDE

| | |
|---|---|
| countryside | campo |
| landscape | paisaje |
| nature | naturaleza |
| view | vista |
| mountain | montaña |
| hill | colina |
| valley | valle |
| river | río |
| stream | arroyo |
| lake | lago |
| forest | bosque |
| farm | granja |

# DAIRY PRODUCTS

| | |
|---|---|
| dairy products | lácteos |
| milk | leche |
| butter | mantequilla |
| margarine | margarina |
| cheese | queso |
| yogurt | yogur |
| cream | nata |
| ice cream | helado |
| milk shake | batido |
| whole milk | leche entera |
| skimmed milk | leche desnatada |

# THE DAY

| | |
|---|---|
| day | día |
| morning | mañana |
| afternoon | tarde |
| evening | tarde |
| night | noche |
| midday | mediodía |
| midnight | medianoche |
| early morning | madrugada |
| early | temprano |
| late | tarde |
| sunrise | salida del sol |
| sunset | puesta del sol |

# DELICATESSEN

| | |
|---|---|
| delicatessen | charcutería |
| cooked meats | fiambres |
| ham | jamón |
| pork loin | lomo |
| spicy sausage | chorizo |
| salami | salami |
| cheese | queso |
| goat's cheese | queso de cabra |
| sheep's cheese | queso de oveja |
| mature cheese | queso curado |
| olives | aceitunas |
| olive oil | aceite de oliva |

# DESSERTS

| | |
|---|---|
| dessert | postre |
| ice cream | helado |
| sorbet | sorbete |
| apple tart | tarta de manzana |
| rice pudding | arroz con leche |
| chocolate mousse | mousse de chocolate |
| crème caramel | flan |
| custard dessert | natillas |
| cheesecake | tarta de queso |

# DIRECTIONS

| | |
|---|---|
| right | derecha |
| left | izquierda |
| straight on | todo recto |
| cross | cruce |
| turn | doble |
| corner | esquina |
| roundabout | rotonda |
| near | cerca |
| far | lejos |
| opposite | enfrente |
| next to | al lado de |
| behind | detrás de |

# DRIVING

| | |
|---|---|
| car | coche |
| driver | conductor |
| licence | carné |
| insurance | seguro |
| registration | matrícula |
| car key | llave del coche |
| seat belt | cinturón |
| roof rack | baca |
| car seat | silla de automóvil |
| breakdown | avería |
| tow truck | grúa |

# DRIVING

| | |
|---|---|
| petrol station | gasolinera |
| diesel | diesel |
| unleaded | sin plomo |
| oil | aceite |
| air | aire |
| water | agua |
| road | carretera |
| dual c/way | autovía |
| motorway | autopista |
| toll | peaje |
| roadworks | obras |
| diversion | desvío |

# DRIVING

| | |
|---|---|
| garage | taller |
| battery | batería |
| tyre | neumático |
| puncture | pinchazo |
| brakes | frenos |
| exhaust pipe | tubo de escape |
| windscreen | parabrisas |
| indicator | intermitente |
| lights | luces |
| door | puerta |
| bonnet | capó |
| boot | maletero |

# ENTERTAINMENT

| | |
|---|---|
| cinema | cine |
| ticket | entrada |
| film | película |
| theatre | teatro |
| music | música |
| concert | concierto |
| show | espectáculo |
| dance | baile |
| disco | discoteca |
| circus | circo |
| funfair | parque de atracciones |

# THE FAMILY

| | |
|---|---|
| family | familia |
| parents | padres |
| father | padre |
| mother | madre |
| son | hijo |
| daughter | hija |
| brother | hermano |
| sister | hermana |
| grandfather | abuelo |
| grandmother | abuela |
| grandson | nieto |
| granddaughter | nieta |

# THE FAMILY

| | |
|---|---|
| uncle | tío |
| aunt | tía |
| nephew | sobrino |
| niece | sobrina |
| cousin | primo |
| husband | marido |
| wife | esposa |
| children | hijos |
| father-in-law | suegro |
| mother-in-law | suegra |
| son-in-law | yerno |
| daughter-in-law | nuera |

# FISH

| | |
|---|---|
| fish | pescado |
| salmon | salmón |
| tuna | atún |
| sardines | sardinas |
| cod | bacalao |
| hake | merluza |
| sole | lenguado |
| monkfish | rape |
| red mullet | salmonete |
| swordfish | pez espada |
| sea bass | lubina |
| sea bream | besugo |

# FOOTBALL

| | |
|---|---|
| football | fútbol |
| footballer | futbolista |
| ball | balón |
| pitch | campo |
| player | jugador |
| team | equipo |
| match | partido |
| stadium | estadio |
| referee | árbitro |
| penalty | penalty |
| corner | córner |
| goal | gol |

# FRUIT

| | |
|---|---|
| fruit | fruta |
| apple | manzana |
| orange | naranja |
| lemon | limón |
| pear | pera |
| banana | plátano |
| grape | uva |
| melon | melón |
| pineapple | piña |
| strawberry | fresa |
| raspberry | frambuesa |
| peach | melocotón |

# GARDEN

| | |
|---|---|
| garden | jardín |
| gardener | jardinero |
| garden centre | viveros |
| grass | césped |
| flowers | flores |
| tree | árbol |
| shrub | arbusto |
| plant | planta |
| soil | tierra |
| fence | valla |
| barbecue | barbacoa |
| awning | toldo |

# HAIR

| | |
|---|---|
| hairdresser's | peluquería |
| hair | pelo |
| brush | cepillo |
| comb | peine |
| shampoo | champú |
| conditioner | suavizante |
| hairspray | laca |
| highlights | reflejos |
| to wash | lavar |
| to cut | cortar |
| to dry | secar |
| to dye | teñir |

# HEALTH

| | |
|---|---|
| health | salud |
| illness | enfermedad |
| cough | tos |
| cold | resfriado |
| sore throat | dolor de garganta |
| flu | gripe |
| fever | fiebre |
| pain | dolor |
| diarrhoea | diarrea |
| constipation | estreñimiento |
| to vomit | vomitar |

# HERBS & SPICES

| | |
|---|---|
| herb | hierba |
| parsley | perejil |
| thyme | tomillo |
| oregano | orégano |
| basil | albahaca |
| sage | salvia |
| spice | especia |
| salt | sal |
| pepper | pimienta |
| paprika | pimentón |
| garlic | ajo |
| saffron | azafrán |

# HOME ENTERTAINMENT

| | |
|---|---|
| television | televisor |
| radio | radio |
| digital | digital |
| satellite | satélite |
| satellite dish | parabólica |
| dvd player | reproductor dvd |
| cd player | reproductor cd |
| hi-fi | equipo hi-fi |
| games console | consola de videojuegos |
| remote control | mando a distancia |

# HOSPITAL

| | |
|---|---|
| hospital | hospital |
| patient | paciente |
| appointment | cita |
| check-up | revisión |
| doctor | médico |
| nurse | enfermero |
| consultant | especialista |
| ward | sala |
| waiting room | sala de espera |
| accident & emergency | urgencias |

# HOTEL

| | |
|---|---|
| hotel | hotel |
| reservation | reserva |
| reception | recepción |
| key | llave |
| bill | cuenta |
| room | habitación |
| single room | individual |
| double room | doble |
| breakfast | desayuno |
| half board | media pensión |
| full board | pensión completa |

# HOTEL

| | |
|---|---|
| dining room | comedor |
| lounge | salón |
| bar | bar |
| lift | ascensor |
| safe | caja fuerte |
| balcony | balcón |
| swimming pool | piscina |
| heating | calefacción |
| air-conditioning | aire acondicionado |
| parking | aparcamiento |
| garage | garaje |

# HOUSE

| | |
|---|---|
| house | casa |
| door | puerta |
| key | llave |
| living room | salón |
| bedroom | dormitorio |
| bathroom | cuarto de baño |
| kitchen | cocina |
| toilet | aseo |
| utility room | lavadero |
| balcony | balcón |
| roof terrace | azotea |
| garden | jardín |

# HOUSE

| | |
|---|---|
| roof | techo |
| stairs | escalera |
| window | ventana |
| blind | persiana |
| alarm | alarma |
| water | agua |
| gas | gas |
| electricity | electricidad |
| heating | calefacción |
| boiler | caldera |
| air-conditioning | aire acondicionado |

# HOUSE REPAIR

| | |
|---|---|
| repair | arreglo |
| maintenance | mantenimiento |
| alteration | reforma |
| builder | albañil |
| electrician | electricista |
| plumber | fontanero |
| carpenter | carpintero |
| locksmith | cerrajero |
| glazier | cristalero |
| painter | pintor |
| ironmonger's | ferretería |
| D.I.Y. | bricolaje |

# JEWELLERY

| | |
|---|---|
| jewellery | joyas |
| jeweller's | joyería |
| watch | reloj |
| ring | anillo |
| necklace | collar |
| bracelet | pulsera |
| brooch | broche |
| earring | pendiente |
| chain | cadena |
| cuff link | gemelo |
| gold | oro |
| silver | plata |

# KITCHEN

| | |
|---|---|
| kitchen | cocina |
| oven | horno |
| hob | placa |
| fridge | frigorífico |
| freezer | congelador |
| washing m/c | lavadora |
| dishwasher | lavavajillas |
| microwave | microondas |
| kettle | hervidor |
| toaster | tostador |
| saucepan | cazo |
| frying pan | sartén |

# KITCHEN

| | |
|---|---|
| crockery | vajilla |
| plate | plato |
| dinner plate | plato llano |
| soup dish | plato hondo |
| cup | taza |
| saucer | platillo |
| teapot | tetera |
| jug | jarra |
| glass | vaso |
| wine glass | copa de vino |
| salad bowl | ensaladera |
| fruit bowl | frutero |

# KITCHEN

| | |
|---|---|
| cutlery | cubiertos |
| knife | cuchillo |
| fork | tenedor |
| spoon | cuchara |
| teaspoon | cucharilla |
| soup spoon | cuchara sopera |
| ladle | cucharón |
| peeler | pelador |
| grater | rallador |
| tin opener | abrelatas |
| bottle opener | abrebotellas |
| corkscrew | sacacorchos |

# THE LAW

| | |
|---|---|
| law | ley |
| lawyer | abogado |
| contract | contrato |
| signature | firma |
| notary | notario |
| deposit | depósito |
| witness | testigo |
| will | testamento |
| house deeds | escritura |
| licence | permiso |
| residence permit | permiso de residencia |

# LIVING ROOM

| | |
|---|---|
| living room | salón |
| sofa | sofá |
| armchair | sillón |
| sideboard | aparador |
| table | mesa |
| chair | silla |
| curtains | cortinas |
| cushion | cojín |
| rug | alfombra |
| picture | cuadro |
| clock | reloj |
| lamp | lámpara |

# MEAT

| | |
|---|---|
| meat | carne |
| steak | bistec |
| fillet steak | solomillo |
| veal | ternera |
| lamb | cordero |
| pork | cerdo |
| chicken | pollo |
| turkey | pavo |
| duck | pato |
| rabbit | conejo |
| chop | chuleta |
| breast | pechuga |

# MONTHS

| | |
|---|---|
| January | enero |
| February | febrero |
| March | marzo |
| April | abril |
| May | mayo |
| June | junio |
| July | julio |
| August | agosto |
| September | septiembre |
| October | octubre |
| November | noviembre |
| December | diciembre |

# NATIONALITIES

| | |
|---|---|
| nationality | nacionalidad |
| British | británico |
| English | inglés |
| Scottish | escocés |
| Welsh | galés |
| Northern Irish | norirlandés |
| Irish | irlandés |
| Spanish | español |
| Portuguese | portugués |
| French | francés |
| German | alemán |
| Italian | italiano |

# NUMBERS

| | |
|---|---|
| number | número |
| zero | cero |
| one | uno |
| two | dos |
| three | tres |
| four | cuatro |
| five | cinco |
| six | seis |
| seven | siete |
| eight | ocho |
| nine | nueve |
| ten | diez |

# NUMBERS

| | |
|---|---|
| eleven | once |
| twelve | doce |
| thirteen | trece |
| fourteen | catorce |
| fifteen | quince |
| sixteen | dieciséis |
| seventeen | diecisiete |
| eighteen | dieciocho |
| nineteen | diecinueve |
| twenty | veinte |
| twenty-one | veintiuno |
| twenty-two | veintidós |

# NUMBERS

| | |
|---|---|
| thirty | treinta |
| forty | cuarenta |
| fifty | cincuenta |
| sixty | sesenta |
| seventy | setenta |
| eighty | ochenta |
| ninety | noventa |
| one hundred | cien |
| two hundred | doscientos |
| five hundred | quinientos |
| thousand | mil |
| million | millón |

# OPTICIAN

| | |
|---|---|
| optician's | óptica |
| eye | ojo |
| eye test | examen de ojos |
| appointment | cita |
| glasses | gafas |
| frame | montura |
| lens | cristal |
| glasses case | estuche |
| short-sighted | miope |
| long-sighted | hipermétrope |
| contact lens | lentilla |
| sunglasses | gafas de sol |

# THE PARK

| | |
|---|---|
| park | parque |
| gardens | jardines |
| grass | césped |
| trees | árboles |
| flowers | flores |
| lake | lago |
| fountain | fuente |
| statue | estatua |
| kiosk | quiosco |
| bench | banco |
| swings | columpios |
| slide | tobogán |

# PEOPLE

| | |
|---|---|
| people | gente |
| man | hombre |
| woman | mujer |
| boy | niño |
| girl | niña |
| children | niños |
| young person | joven |
| pensioner | pensionista |
| friend | amigo |
| boyfriend | novio |
| girlfriend | novia |
| neighbour | vecino |

# PERSONAL DETAILS

| | |
|---|---|
| name | nombre |
| surname | apellido |
| address | domicilio |
| postcode | código postal |
| telephone | teléfono |
| male | varón |
| female | mujer |
| married | casado |
| single | soltero |
| age | edad |
| date of birth | fecha de nacimiento |

# THE POLICE

| | |
|---|---|
| police | policía |
| police station | comisaría |
| police officer | agente de policía |
| legal | legal |
| illegal | ilegal |
| accident | accidente |
| witness | testigo |
| statement | declaración |
| offence | delito |
| fine | multa |
| theft | robo |

# THE PORT

| | |
|---|---|
| port | puerto |
| boat | barco |
| yacht | yate |
| ferry | ferry |
| fishing port | puerto pesquero |
| fishing boat | barca pesquera |
| fish market | lonja |
| yacht club | club náutico |
| marina | puerto deportivo |

# POST OFFICE

| | |
|---|---|
| post office | Correos |
| postman | cartero |
| postbox | buzón |
| letter | carta |
| envelope | sobre |
| stamp | sello |
| address | dirección |
| postcode | código postal |
| airmail | por avión |
| parcel | paquete |
| fragile | frágil |
| urgent | urgente |

# PUBLIC TRANSPORT

| | |
|---|---|
| airport | aeropuerto |
| taxi | taxi |
| bus | autobús |
| train | tren |
| underground | metro |
| timetable | horario |
| ticket office | taquilla |
| ticket | billete |
| single | ida |
| return | ida y vuelta |
| platform | andén |
| left-luggage | consigna |

# READING

| | |
|---|---|
| bookshop | librería |
| kiosk | quiosco |
| library | biblioteca |
| newspaper | periódico |
| magazine | revista |
| comic | tebeo |
| book | libro |
| novel | novela |
| guide book | guía |
| dictionary | diccionario |
| phrase book | guía de conversación |

# RESTAURANT

| | |
|---|---|
| restaurant | restaurante |
| reservation | reserva |
| waiter | camarero |
| dining room | comedor |
| terrace | terraza |
| lunch | almuerzo |
| dinner | cena |
| menu | carta |
| set menu | menú del día |
| wine list | carta de vinos |
| bill | cuenta |
| toilets | servicios |

# RESTAURANT

| | |
|---|---|
| bread | pan |
| starters | entradas |
| soup | sopa |
| salad | ensalada |
| meat | carnes |
| fish | pescados |
| seafood | mariscos |
| rice dishes | arroces |
| dessert | postres |
| still water | agua sin gas |
| sparkling water | agua con gas |

# SALAD

| | |
|---|---|
| salad | ensalada |
| lettuce | lechuga |
| tomato | tomate |
| onion | cebolla |
| cucumber | pepino |
| pepper | pimiento |
| olives | aceitunas |
| asparagus | espárrago |
| avocado | aguacate |
| radish | rábano |
| beetroot | remolacha |
| celery | apio |

# SCHOOL

| | |
|---|---|
| school | colegio |
| teacher | profesor |
| pupil | alumno |
| class | clase |
| classroom | aula |
| timetable | horario |
| course | curso |
| term | trimestre |
| text book | libro de texto |
| homework | deberes |
| exam | examen |
| holiday | vacaciones |

# SEAFOOD

| | |
|---|---|
| seafood | mariscos |
| prawns | gambas |
| king prawn | langostino |
| lobster | langosta |
| mussels | mejillones |
| clams | almejas |
| oyster | ostra |
| scallops | vieiras |
| squid | calamares |
| octopus | pulpo |
| cuttlefish | sepia |
| crab | cangrejo |

# SHOES

| | |
|---|---|
| shoe shop | zapatería |
| footwear | calzado |
| shoe | zapato |
| boot | bota |
| trainer | zapatilla de deporte |
| sandal | sandalia |
| flip-flop | chancla |
| slipper | zapatilla |
| shoe polish | betún |
| heel | tacón |
| sole | suela |

# SHOPPING

| | |
|---|---|
| shop | tienda |
| size | talla |
| price | precio |
| receipt | recibo |
| till | caja |
| sale | rebajas |
| discount | descuento |
| changing room | probador |
| department store | grandes almacenes |
| shopping centre | centro comercial |

# SIGHTSEEING

| | |
|---|---|
| tourist office | oficina de turismo |
| information | información |
| town map | plano |
| places of interest | lugares de interés |
| timetable | horario |
| guide book | guía |
| ticket | entrada |
| excursion | excursión |
| souvenir | recuerdo |
| postcard | postal |

# SIGHTSEEING

| | |
|---|---|
| main square | plaza mayor |
| palace | palacio |
| castle | castillo |
| cathedral | catedral |
| church | iglesia |
| museum | museo |
| monument | monumento |
| park | parque |
| gardens | jardines |
| stadium | estadio |
| river | río |
| view | vista |

# SIGNS

| | |
|---|---|
| entrance | entrada |
| exit | salida |
| push | empujar |
| pull | tirar |
| for sale | se vende |
| for rent | se alquila |
| out of order | no funciona |
| danger | peligro |
| no smoking | prohibido fumar |
| no parking | prohibido aparcar |

# SNACKS

| | |
|---|---|
| bar snacks | tapas |
| portion | ración |
| half portion | media ración |
| ham | jamón |
| cheese | queso |
| prawns | gambas |
| croquettes | croquetas |
| meatballs | albóndigas |
| Spanish omelette | tortilla de patatas |
| spicy potatoes | patatas bravas |
| Russian salad | ensaladilla rusa |

# SOFT DRINKS

| | |
|---|---|
| soft drink | refresco |
| juice | zumo |
| orange | naranja |
| lemon | limón |
| pineapple | piña |
| peach | melocotón |
| lemonade | gaseosa |
| ice | hielo |
| crushed ice drink | granizado |
| fresh orange juice | zumo de naranja natural |

# SPIRITS

| | |
|---|---|
| spirits | licores |
| whisky | whisky |
| gin | ginebra |
| vodka | vodka |
| rum | ron |
| brandy | brandy |
| soda | soda |
| tonic | tónica |
| ginger ale | ginger ale |
| lemonade | gaseosa |
| water | agua |
| ice | hielo |

# SPORT

| | |
|---|---|
| sport | deporte |
| sports centre | polideportivo |
| changing room | vestuario |
| football | fútbol |
| rugby | rugby |
| tennis | tenis |
| golf | golf |
| basketball | baloncesto |
| volleyball | vóleibol |
| squash | squash |
| swimming | natación |
| sailing | vela |

# STATIONERY

| | |
|---|---|
| stationer's | papelería |
| paper | papel |
| pen | bolígrafo |
| pencil | lápiz |
| ink | tinta |
| envelope | sobre |
| folder | carpeta |
| notebook | cuaderno |
| diary | agenda |
| photocopy | fotocopia |
| fax | fax |
| laminated | plastificado |

# SUPERMARKET

| | |
|---|---|
| supermarket | supermercado |
| meat | carnes |
| fish | pescados |
| fruit | frutas |
| vegetables | verduras |
| dairy products | lácteos |
| delicatessen | charcutería |
| bakery | panadería |
| frozen food | congelados |
| tinned food | conservas |
| drinks | bebidas |
| wines | vinos |

# SUPERMARKET

| | |
|---|---|
| tea | té |
| coffee | café |
| milk | leche |
| sugar | azúcar |
| bread | pan |
| butter | mantequilla |
| margarine | margarina |
| jam | mermelada |
| honey | miel |
| cereals | cereales |
| juice | zumo |
| water | agua |

# SUPERMARKET

| | |
|---|---|
| eggs | huevos |
| bacon | bacon |
| sausage | salchicha |
| sauce | salsa |
| ketchup | ketchup |
| mayonnaise | mahonesa |
| mustard | mostaza |
| soup | sopa |
| rice | arroz |
| salt | sal |
| pepper | pimienta |
| oil | aceite |

# SUPERMARKET

| | |
|---|---|
| tissues | pañuelos |
| nappy | pañal |
| toilet roll | papel higiénico |
| kitchen roll | rollo de cocina |
| detergent | detergente |
| softener | suavizante |
| bleach | lejía |
| polish | cera |
| batteries | pilas |
| light bulb | bombilla |
| washing-up liquid | lavavajillas |

# SWIMMING

| | |
|---|---|
| swimming | natación |
| swimming pool | piscina |
| swimwear | bañadores |
| cap | gorro de baño |
| float | flotador |
| snorkel | esnórkel |
| goggles | gafas de natación |
| changing room | vestuario |
| shower | ducha |
| towel | toalla |
| lifeguard | socorrista |

# TEA & COFFEE

| | |
|---|---|
| tea | té |
| milk | leche |
| sugar | azúcar |
| herbal tea | infusión |
| mint tea | menta poleo |
| camomile tea | manzanilla |
| coffee | café |
| white coffee | café con leche |
| black coffee | café americano |
| espresso | café solo |
| cappuccino | capuchino |
| decaffeinated | descafeinado |

# TELEPHONE

| | |
|---|---|
| telephone | teléfono |
| number | número |
| call | llamada |
| message | mensaje |
| answerphone | contestador |
| coin | moneda |
| phone card | tarjeta telefónica |
| landline | teléfono fijo |
| mobile | móvil |
| SIM card | tarjeta SIM |
| top-up card | tarjeta prepago |

# TIME

| | |
|---|---|
| second | segundo |
| minute | minuto |
| hour | hora |
| quarter hour | cuarto de hora |
| half hour | media hora |
| day | día |
| week | semana |
| weekend | fin de semana |
| working day | día laborable |
| fortnight | quincena |
| month | mes |
| year | año |

# TOILETRIES

| | |
|---|---|
| soap | jabón |
| shampoo | champú |
| conditioner | suavizante |
| shower gel | gel de ducha |
| deodorant | desodorante |
| antiperspirant | antitranspirante |
| moisturizer | crema hidratante |
| toothpaste | pasta de dientes |
| safety razor | maquinilla de afeitar |

# UTILITY ROOM

| | |
|---|---|
| utility room | lavadero |
| mop | fregona |
| bucket | cubo |
| cloth | trapo |
| dustpan | recogedor |
| brush | cepillo |
| clothes airer | tendedero |
| iron | plancha |
| ironing board | tabla de planchar |
| washing machine | lavadora |

# VEGETABLES

| | |
|---|---|
| vegetables | verduras |
| potato | patata |
| carrot | zanahoria |
| onion | cebolla |
| cauliflower | coliflor |
| cabbage | col |
| peas | guisantes |
| spinach | espinaca |
| broccoli | brócoli |
| aubergine | berenjena |
| courgette | calabacín |
| mushrooms | champiñones |

# WEATHER

| | |
|---|---|
| weather | tiempo |
| forecast | pronóstico |
| temperature | temperatura |
| heat | calor |
| sunny | soleado |
| hot | caluroso |
| cold | frío |
| cool | fresco |
| cloudy | nuboso |
| rain | lluvia |
| wind | viento |
| storm | tormenta |

# WEIGHTS & MEASURES

| | |
|---|---|
| weight | peso |
| gram | gramo |
| kilo | kilo |
| half kilo | medio kilo |
| length | longitud |
| centimetre | centímetro |
| metre | metro |
| kilometre | kilómetro |
| height | altura |
| width | anchura |
| depth | profundidad |
| litre | litro |

# WINE

| | |
|---|---|
| wine | vino |
| red wine | vino tinto |
| white wine | vino blanco |
| rosé wine | vino rosado |
| sparkling wine | cava |
| champagne | champán |
| sherry | jerez |
| port | oporto |
| sweet | dulce |
| dry | seco |
| glass | copa |
| bottle | botella |

# THE YEAR

| | |
|---|---|
| year | año |
| spring | primavera |
| summer | verano |
| autumn | otoño |
| winter | invierno |
| Christmas | Navidad |
| New Year | Año Nuevo |
| Christmas Eve | Nochebuena |
| New Year's Eve | Nochevieja |
| Easter week | Semana Santa |
| public holiday | día festivo |
| holiday | vacaciones |

# SPANISH SOUNDS

## Spanish Pronunciation

## Spanish Word Stress

# Spanish Pronunciation

## .ce

In Spanish ce is pronounced like the th in thanks.

Practise saying this th sound with these Spanish words.

| | |
|---|---|
| cerca | near |
| cero | zero |
| cerdo | pig |
| centro | centre |
| cesta | basket |

# Spanish Pronunciation

## .ci

In Spanish ci is pronounced like the th in thanks.

Practise saying this th sound with these Spanish words.

| | |
|---|---|
| cinco | five |
| cita | appointment |
| cien | one hundred |
| circo | circus |
| circular | circular |

# Spanish Pronunciation

## .e

In Spanish e at the end of a word is pronounced like a- the first letter of the English alphabet.

Practise saying this a sound with these Spanish words.

| | |
|---|---|
| madre | mother |
| padre | father |
| coche | car |
| leche | milk |
| grande | big |

# Spanish Pronunciation

## .ge

In Spanish ge is pronounced like the ch in the Scottish word loch. This is a back-of-the-throat sound as if clearing the throat!

Practise saying this throaty loch sound with these Spanish words.

general     general

generoso    generous

genial     brilliant

gente      people

gel        gel

# Spanish Pronunciation

## .gi

In Spanish gi is pronounced like the ch in the Scottish word loch. This is a back-of-the-throat sound as if clearing the throat!

Practise saying this throaty loch sound with these Spanish words.

| | |
|---|---|
| ginebra | gin |
| gimnasta | gymnast |
| gimnasio | gym |
| gitano | gypsy |
| gira | tour |

# Spanish Pronunciation

## .h

In Spanish h has no sound.
It is a silent letter.

Practise saying these Spanish
words making sure h has no
sound.

| | |
|---|---|
| hola | hello |
| hora | hour |
| hoy | today |
| hombre | man |
| hospital | hospital |

# Spanish Pronunciation

## .j

In Spanish j is pronounced like the ch in the Scottish word loch. This is a back-of-the-throat sound as if clearing the throat!

Practise saying this throaty loch sound with these Spanish words.

| | |
|---|---|
| jamón | ham |
| jardín | garden |
| jarra | jug |
| junio | June |
| julio | July |

# Spanish Pronunciation

## ll

In Spanish ll is pronounced like the y in yes.

Practise saying this y sound with these Spanish words.

| | |
|---|---|
| tortilla | omelette |
| castillo | castle |
| cuchillo | knife |
| botella | bottle |
| caballo | horse |

# Spanish Pronunciation

## .ñ

In Spanish ñ is pronounced like ny in canyon.

Practise saying this ny sound with these Spanish words.

| | |
|---|---|
| España | Spain |
| mañana | tomorrow |
| montaña | mountain |
| piña | pineapple |
| Señorita | Miss |

# Spanish Pronunciation

## .V

In Spanish v at the beginning of a word is pronounced like b in big.

Practise saying this b sound with these Spanish words.

| | |
|---|---|
| vino | wine |
| verano | summer |
| verde | green |
| vaso | glass |
| vale | okay |

# Spanish Pronunciation

## .z

In Spanish z is pronounced like the th in thanks.

Practise saying this th sound with these Spanish words.

| | |
|---|---|
| zumo | juice |
| zapato | shoe |
| zona | area |
| plaza | square |
| taza | cup |

# Spanish Pronunciation

# Summary

ce, ci and z is th in thanks

e at the end of a word is a –
the sound of the first letter
of the English alphabet.

ge, gi and j is ch in loch

h is silent

ll is y in yes

ñ is ny in canyon

v at the start of a word is b in big

# Spanish Pronunciation

## Word Stress

Spanish words are normally stressed on the last syllable.

actor  normal  papel  popular

But if a Spanish word ends in a, e, i, o, u, s or n the stress is on the last-but-one syllable.

nota  arte  plato  intenso

If a Spanish word has an accent ( ´ ) the stress is on the accent.

bebé  melón  adiós  teléfono

# SPAIN

## The Highlights
## of Spain


## Maps:
## Mainland Spain
## and
## Spanish Islands

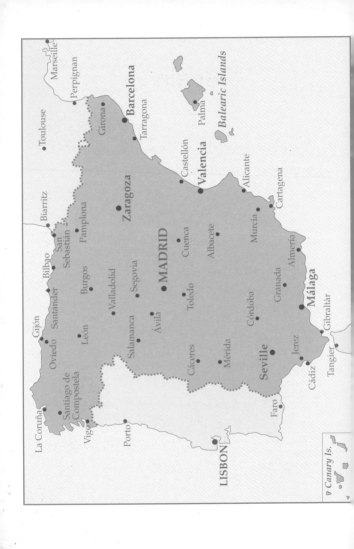

# Spain

Spain is a fantastic country. Millions of people visit every year to enjoy the excellent climate, superb beaches, great facilities and the relaxed way of life.

Spain also has wonderful towns and cities, beautiful scenery and some of the most enjoyable festivals anywhere in Europe.

In the next few pages we have described the different regions of Spain and highlighted our favourite places to visit. We have also recommended the best food and drink available in each region.

# Southern Spain

Andalucía covers all of southern Spain and runs for over 350 miles from the Portuguese  border in the west to the province of Almería in the east. Andalucía is a beautiful and popular region of Spain.

There are excellent beaches all along the coastline. The best beaches are on the Atlantic coast of the Costa de la Luz and along the Mediterranean coast of Almería. Inland there are dramatic mountain ranges and beautiful landscapes.

The cities of Granada, Córdoba and Seville have some of the most interesting and important monuments in Europe and are great places to visit. Andalucía is also famous for some of the most colourful and exciting festivals held in Spain.

# Highlights of Southern Spain

## Places to Visit

Granada's Alhambra palace and gardens. Córdoba's Mezquita mosque and the old town. Seville's Alcázar palace and gardens, Giralda tower and old town. The attractive towns and cities of Cádiz, Jerez and Ronda.

## Food and Drink

| | |
|---|---|
| chilled soups | gazpacho & salmorejo |
| fried fish | fritura de pescado |
| cured ham | jamón ibérico |
| bar snacks | tapas |
| | |
| draught beer | caña |
| dry sherry | fino & manzanilla |
| fruit punch | sangría |
| red wine & lemonade | tinto de verano |

# Eastern Spain

Eastern Spain consists of the regions of Cataluña, Valencia and Murcia. This large region stretches for over 500 miles from the French border in the north to Andalucía in the south.

This region has some of the best scenery in Spain. The Costa Brava, the area around Dénia and the Mar Menor are exceptionally beautiful. The east coast is home to some of the best known holiday resorts in Spain attracting millions of visitors because of the excellent climate, great beaches and superb facilities.

Barcelona is the cultural and commercial capital of Cataluña and one of the best cities in Europe. Valencia and Murcia are also important and attractive regional capitals.

# Highlights of Eastern Spain

## Places to Visit

Barcelona's Sagrada Familia cathedral, Gaudi's buildings and Park Güell, the old town and La Rambla. Valencia's historic centre and City of Arts and Sciences. Alicante's beach, seafront and marina. The attractive centres of Gerona, Murcia, Elche and Cartagena.

## Food and Drink

| | |
|---|---|
| paella & rice dishes | arroces |
| shellfish & noodles | fideuá |
| Catalan sausage | butifarra |
| fresh salad | ensalada |
| fresh fruit | fruta del tiempo |
| | |
| sparkling wine | cava |
| white wines | Penedés region |
| red wines | Priorato region |
| rosé wines | Ampurdán |

# Northern Spain

Northern Spain includes the regions of Galicia, Asturias, Cantabria, the Basque Country and Navarra. It runs for 350 miles from the Atlantic in the west to the Pyrenees in the east. This area has a cooler and wetter climate than the rest of the country and is sometimes called "Green Spain".

The coastline of Galicia is especially beautiful and there are excellent beaches all along the north coast. The mountains of the Picos de Europa and the Spanish Pyrenees have some of the best scenery in Spain.

This region hosts the beautiful resorts of San Sebastián and Santander and the attractive cities of Santiago de Compostela, Oviedo and La Coruña. Bilbao is home to the fantastic Guggenheim Museum.

# Highlights of Northern Spain

## Places to Visit

Santiago de Compostela's cathedral and old town. San Sebastián's bay, beaches and headlands. Santander's bays and beaches. Oviedo's old town.

The stunning coastline of Galicia.

## Food and Drink

| | |
|---|---|
| fresh fish | pescados |
| seafood | mariscos |
| tuna pie | empanada de atún |
| bean stew | fabada asturiana |
| blue cheese | cabrales |
| | |
| white wines | Albariño, Ribeiro, Rías Baixas |
| cider | sidra |
| liqueur | orujo |

# Central Spain

Central Spain covers a huge area from Andalucía in the south to Asturias and Cantabria in the north, from the Portuguese border in the west to Cataluña, Valencia and Murcia in the east. To the south of Madrid there is Castille La Mancha and Extremadura and to the north Castille and León, La Rioja and Aragón.

This massive plain has incredible blue skies throughout the year and is only broken up by mountain ranges to the north and west of Madrid.

Spain's fantastic capital city is in the centre of this region and almost exactly in the centre of Spain. Around Madrid cities like Salamanca, Segovia, Toledo and Ávila are some of the most historic and beautiful cities in Spain.

# Highlights of Central Spain

## Places to Visit

Madrid's Plaza Mayor, Royal Palace and the Thyssen, Prado and Reina Sofía museums. The Retiro Park and gardens. León's cathedral and old town. Salamanca's Plaza Mayor and old town. Ávila's city walls and historic centre. Segovia's Alcázar and aqueduct. Toledo's cathedral, historic centre and El Greco paintings.

## Food and Drink

| | |
|---|---|
| roast lamb | cordero asado |
| suckling pig | cochinillo asado |
| ratatouille | pisto manchego |
| ham | jamón ibérico |
| cheese | queso manchego |
| | |
| red wines | Rioja, Ribera del Duero |
| white wines | Rueda, Rioja |

# The Spanish Islands

Spain has two groups of islands, the Balearic Islands in the Mediterranean and the Canary Islands off the coast of Morocco in the Atlantic.

The Balearic Islands consist of Mallorca, Menorca, Ibiza and Formentera.
The Balearics have stunning coastlines, beautiful coves, excellent beaches and some of the best tourist facilities in Europe. Palma de Mallorca, Ibiza and Mahón are lively and attractive capital cities.

The Canary Islands are Gran Canaria, Lanzarote, Fuerteventura, Tenerife, La Gomera, El Hierro and La Palma.
The Canaries have an excellent year round climate, dramatic volcanic landscapes, some excellent beaches and vibrant capital cities in Las Palmas de Gran Canaria and Santa Cruz de Tenerife.

# Highlights of the Islands

## Places to Visit

Balearics - Palma, Ibiza, Mahón and Ciutadella. The beaches of northern Mallorca, southern Menorca and Ibiza. Canaries - Las Palmas, Santa Cruz de Tenerife. The beaches of Gran Canaria and Fuerteventura. Volcanic landscapes in Lanzarote and Tenerife.

## Food and Drink

Balearics
| | |
|---|---|
| breakfast pastry | ensaimada |
| Menorcan cheese | queso de Mahón |
| local wine | Binissalem |

Canaries
| | |
|---|---|
| fresh fish | pescados |
| salted potatoes | papas arrugadas |
| spicy sauce | mojo colorado |
| rum | ron |

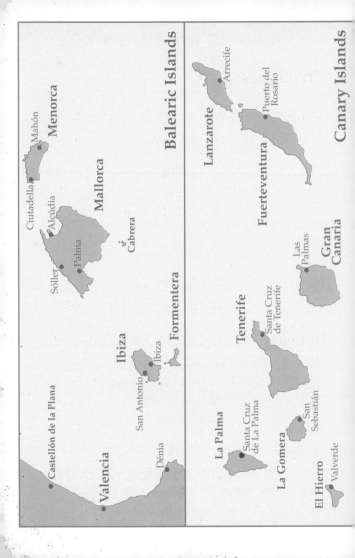

**Balearic Islands**

Menorca
Mahón
Ciutadella
Alcúdia
Mallorca
Sóller
Palma
Cabrera

Ibiza
San Antonio
Ibiza
Formentera

Castellón de la Plana
Dénia
Valencia

**Canary Islands**

Lanzarote
Arrecife
Puerto del Rosario
Fuerteventura

Gran Canaria
Las Palmas

Tenerife
Santa Cruz de Tenerife

La Palma
Santa Cruz de La Palma
San Sebastián
La Gomera
El Hierro
Valverde

# Index